FEEL FREE TO KEEP QUOTING ME

365 more days of musings, mishaps,
and misshapen observations.

The Captain

Ashley, let's try this again.

JANUARY 1

I like my mornings to be slow and quiet.
I want the day to romance me a bit
before it tries to fuck me.

You don't have to explain yourself to everyone. Whether people understand you or not is not your problem. Does a leopard have to explain its spots? No. It just sits there looking fucking hot.

"Control your emotions" doesn't mean "avoid your emotions." Feel your shit, understand your shit, but don't lose your shit.

Maybe it's not that you haven't found
the one and it's the fact that you
haven't actually become someone
who can be the one to someone else.
Seriously, get your shit together.

No matter how attractive somebody is — if their attitude is negative and shitty — avoid them. They're human lava: Hot, but they slowly destroy everything around them.

When shit gets weird, try not to react out of fear. A fearful reaction is a missed opportunity for a meaningful, perhaps educational, interaction. We learn from the situations that scare us — so, let's look forward to seeing what other fucked-up things life has waiting for us.

A sense of humor is critical to your survival. Sure, you need food, water, shelter, and other stuff like that — but a sense of humor is what holds your shit together when life is being a motherfucker.

Dress to impress. As in, impress yourself by dressing fucking ridiculous to see if you can still get the job, free entry, or a second date. Maybe you'll surprise yourself with the fact that your personality is far cooler than you had thought previously.

Integrity is sexy. Those who have it, wear it well. Those who lack it, I hope to repel. And, to those who don't even know what it is, look it up after reading this — because you don't fucking have it.

In life, you have to find yourself.
Nobody else should do this for you.
Besides, where's the fun in being found
by someone? Even as a child you knew
this was a bad idea; only the kids who
fucking sucked at Hide-and-Seek
would allow that to happen.

If you can believe in ghosts, horoscopes, and magical crystals, why can't you believe in yourself? Are you seriously telling me that you have more faith in a fucking rock than you do your own mind?

So much of life is simply being able to confidently suck, fuck up, or make the most of seemingly bad luck. Attitude is everything — especially when you're terrible at a lot of things.

The fondest memory of my childhood: If you didn't like somebody, you had to say it to their face. You couldn't just leave a comment. You had to actually walk up and say, "Brandon, you can't come to my 9th birthday party because you're an asshole."

Dogs are living proof that humor and personality are more important than looks and money. It doesn't matter how broke or ugly a dog is, if he's fun to have around, she wants to have him around. That's good news for some of you dudes.

Time committed shouldn't justify future time wasted. You wouldn't continue eating food that tastes like shit — so why continue stressing over something that's not a good fit? You tried. Now, move on and stop putting things in your mouth and mind that don't fucking belong.

Your energy is more valuable than your time; something that only takes minutes, can drain you for hours or days. And, well, some people are the energy-sucking equivalent of getting in a fucking car accident.

Imagine how differently everybody would treat each other if the "you break it, you buy it" rule applied to people. Well, pretend it does and stop being a fucking asshole.

Growing up is not a trap. Peter Pan was a joke and he only had friends because he could fly. So, unless you also want to be friends with a bunch of lost boys who only like you when your life is flying high, grow up and give "adulting" a try.

Dating is a lot like dog training: If you don't set boundaries and stick to them, get used to dealing with shit, losing sleep, and constantly protecting your food from fucking thieves.

You should pursue everything in life that is new and unknown to you. This is the only way to truly experience living. Just avoid the shit that will put you in prison.

A lack of compatibility isn't
something to be taken personally.
Here's the deal: Some people won't
fucking like you, some people won't
want to fuck you, and some people
will simply think you fucking suck;
but — what others think of you —
isn't a reason to stop being you.

Skin is your body's largest organ because it has such an important role: protecting you from the world. And, you can help your skin grow thicker and do its job more effectively by not taking everything so personally.

If sugarcoated conversations solved problems, that mouth of yours would be worth something. Stop lying to yourself and others about how you feel. Then, watch how quickly your life begins to feel less problematic and more manageable.

You should want a woman who's hands-on, but also a handful. Like, she'll take an active role in helping you become a better person — but she'll do this by testing every bit of your fucking patience.

Understand your past, but treat it like an uninvited guest at the party that is your present life: "Hey, who's that creepy-ass guy in the corner?" "Oh, that's just my past. Don't worry, he won't bother us."

It's not easy being yourself, but it becomes a hell of a lot easier when you put your happiness before your popularity. I mean, if you truly believe "everybody sucks" — why do you value their sucky opinions so fucking much?

Mental health is a motherfucker. And, not talking about it doesn't make you tougher; it prolongs the amount of time that you'll fucking suffer. So, you can disregard this stupid rhyme (and that's fine) — but whatever you do — don't ignore the pain within your own mind.

The more you change yourself for somebody else, the further you separate from your true self. And, the last thing you should want is to be here on Earth, dating a jerk, while the best version of you is floating around lost in fucking space.

Whether it's your work life, sex life,
or just your everyday life, learning
to be happy for others when they
get something will dramatically
change your life.

Self-importance is self-sabotage. The moment you begin to get too high on your own hype, is the same moment you set a lower standard for your life. So, unless you plan to stay exactly where you are at today, do yourself a favor and stop acting like you're some kind of savior.

Intuition is great because it helps you see through others' bullshit, but self-awareness is more valuable because it helps you see through the bullshit you tell yourself.

If you're worried you don't have
the strength to move on, think
of how much strength you are
using to hold on — then, redirect
that energy and enjoy your life.

Sometimes, you have to cut your losses;
other times, you have to trust the process.
Giving up on a dream too early is like
leaving an orgy still feeling horny: Don't
let a small inconvenience, or a sudden
lack of confidence, prevent you from
finishing what you fucking started.

Fear regret more than you fear commitment. Because if you truly care — the words left unsaid, the acts left undone, and the love left unsung — will fuck with you way more than sharing a bed, a bathroom, or breadsticks with someone.

Learning to let go and let life unfold has nothing to do with giving up. It simply means, sometimes, instead of figuring it out, you have to wait it out. Feel it don't force it. Patience not pressure. And, most importantly, dignity not desperation.

Passion is the purest form of creation.
Because when you're passionate about
something — anything that's positive —
an insane amount of creativity is possible.
Sadly, too many people are passionate
about dumb shit and drama.

In times of uncertainty, stress is your motherfucking enemy. So, with all the instability that you currently feel, controlling your mentality is what's ultimately going to help you deal.

All-or-nothing thinking leads to an
overall lack of action and understanding.
You're not always going to get things
100% right — but that doesn't mean
you're 100% wrong — the important
thing is that you're using your thinking
to at least do something.

You need at least one person in your life who can — and will — fucking check you. (And this person can't be yourself because you have no idea how arrogant, absurd, or annoying you are sometimes.)

Your honesty is all you can truly promise anybody. It's the only thing you can absolutely control in any situation. So, be true to yourself — and straightforward with others — and let the universe handle all of the bullshit that remains confusing and undiscovered.

Self-awareness is the first step in emotional preparedness. Seriously, until you fully understand how goddamn fucking crazy you are, you can't accurately let other people know what to prepare for.

Don't let exhaustion keep you from exploring your options. Whether it's sex, searching for your purpose, or simply surviving a weird fucking year — don't stop trying new things just because too much of the same thing has you feeling too tired to do so.

If you can find happiness even when shit happens, your life is headed in the right direction. Because shit will happen, but it will feel like shitty shit happens more often when you're only looking for problems.

You don't want a puzzle that is assembled; the fun part is putting it together. Likewise, if you think you need everything in place in order to enjoy your life, you're missing the point of living and you'll be dead before you even come close to getting your shit together.

VALENTINE'S DAY

The same people who talk
shit about Valentine's Day will
celebrate their birthday for an
entire fucking month because
they're only capable of thinking
about themselves.

Sometimes, people will suggest you fix things about yourself, not because they want to help you, but because they want you to help them be more comfortable around you. Watch out for that shit; then, tell whomever it is, "If you're looking for comfort, go buy a fucking blanket."

That's cool that you refuse to use plastic straws because you want to protect the ocean, but what about all the shit that's polluting your mind because you're listening to the wrong opinions?

Your life is going to change; the least you can do is decide for yourself what some of those changes are going to be. You wouldn't allow a complete stranger to choose your new haircut, so why sit back and wait for others to make the kind of decisions that can really fuck you up?

Give yourself some credit. You might not be exactly where you want to be in life right now — but, goddamnit, at least you're not on a reality TV show as one of a dozen losers all wasting your time trying to date the same individual.

The overconsumption of media leads to patterns of thinking that lack value and meaning. If you don't think for yourself, how will you ever know yourself? Far too many people have literally no fucking idea who they are because they only think and believe what they hear and see.

Too many people are playing Freeze Tag with their fucking life, allowing the past actions of another to leave them frozen, waiting for somebody else to come along and fucking save 'em. Forget what happened, fight the urge to feel self-pity, and unfreeze your fucking self already.

Venom is injected; poison is absorbed. People will spew venom at you — but without a wound — it can't affect you. You have to allow the poison of their words to seep into you. Basically, having thick skin is your immunity to negativity and stupidity.

You can learn more from listening to a gut feeling than you ever could from a book, a speech, or a meeting. If you're looking for advice, start with yourself — listen and learn. And, if somebody tries to interrupt your personal conversation, tell them to wait their fucking turn.

Moments of self-doubt help you discover what you're all about. Think back on all the times you overcame something that seemed impossible. Then, remind yourself that getting through Monday is just another bitch-ass obstacle for you to topple.

I want a girl who's genuine, but also a degenerate. Like, when necessary, she'll speak with heartfelt sincerity — but the rest of the time — she's a funny, vulgar, sarcastic asshole.

When the common enemy is
stupidity, there will always
be a division in society.

Dating can sometimes feel like wearing a jacket in the summertime: Initially, it seems like a great idea; but, eventually, the sweat, discomfort, and overall annoyance begins to outweigh whatever positive contributions it has to your life/outfit.

Life hacks are getting ridiculous:
"Turn your old clothing into curtains
as hideous as your personality."
"Collect wine corks until you have
enough to build a small raft and sail
away from your problems." "Use your
ex as an excuse for everything that's
fucked up about yourself."

A fragile ego is the sign of a closed mind. Once you open yourself up to the idea that everyone is entitled to their own opinion, you'll no longer give a fuck about your own ideas being brought into question.

I like how people panic every
time a social media platform
changes. Relax, you're still going
to be able to post the same boring
comments and photos you've
been sharing for years.

There will always be something in life you will wish you had done or said differently — but dwelling on these — will keep you from focusing on what you're doing and saying now. And, you really should focus. Because you're probably about to do or say something stupid.

Complacency is contagious.
Use your goals like a condom
and protect yourself from
those who are content living a
life of boredom.

I wish personalities had a fragrance. You could sniff out if someone's sweet, sour, or a pile of burning garbage before even talking to them — like a scented candle of friendship potential.

Hold yourself accountable, but not unforgivable. Replace your inner dialogue of blame with a dialogue of change and every mistake, fuck-up, or misfortune becomes a part of the learning process — instead of another reason to hate yourself because you lack self-forgiveness.

From time to time, everyone
feels inadequate; what separates
professionals from amateurs is
how you choose to deal with it. You
can work, or you can complain. One
makes you better; the other leaves
you the exact fucking same.

Living is less about "what," and more about "who" and "where." It's not about what you can purchase and possess; it's about where you go and who you meet along the way. Even meeting someone utterly fucking sucky can provide you with another valuable life story.

3 A.M. is known as the "Devil's
Hour" because that's when ghosts,
witches, and demons are most likely
to appear. It also happens to be the
time when you're most likely to
receive a "U up?" text. Coincidence?
I think not. Beware of those devil
dicks and haunted holes, my friends.

Forget about your "summer body." You think bears come out of hibernation worrying about how they're going to look in August? Hell no — they eat, mate, and enjoy life.

Let your behavior be something that others can't help but savor. Everything you do or say can easily become the highlight of somebody's day. Likewise, you can quickly make someone feel sick when you choose to be a dumb fucking dick.

You ever fuck up a word so badly that autocorrect can't figure out what you're trying to say, but you just send it anyway? That's kind of how you should live your life: Sometimes, you just have to hit send on your decision, regardless of somebody else's misunderstanding or opinion.

If you take life too seriously, there's a good chance you're going to miss out entirely. It's okay to let loose, let live, and let yourself off the hook every once in a while — just don't let go. Rose did that back in '97 and nobody has forgotten about it.

Accomplish goals for your own satisfaction. Acknowledgment from others is a bonus, not the purpose. You're going to do a lot of cool shit in life that will go completely unnoticed. And, you'll do a lot of embarrassing shit that many will see. Only your self-action is guaranteed.

Fresh starts are all around you. And, the change doesn't even have to be that drastic to have real impact. Take a shower, eat some vegetables — tell someone toxic to stop fucking texting you.

Procrastination is self-inflicted
punishment. When you waste precious
time, you rob yourself of peace of mind.
With that said, seen anything lately on
Netflix that you'd recommend?

There's power in everything you devour. The food you eat, the books you read, the people you allow to fill your holes and life with negative-ass energy — if you let it in you, it becomes you. So, load yourself up carefully.

Second-guessing only prevents you from progressing. Once you've made a decision, fucking live with it and focus on what you're going to do next; redefine FOMO as "Focus On Moving On" and stop worrying about shit that you've already left — like people, plans, and lame-ass parties.

Not everything in life is black and white — too far in any direction is close-minded and misguided. Relax, not every comment is a personal attack. Live your life in color; you'll be surprised by all the cool shit that you uncover. Hell, you might even find a sense of fucking humor.

We need an adults-only airport with every sign written in stressed-out, frustrated airport language: "There's a fucking bar this way." "Turn left for the pizza you fucking need right now." "Never been through security? Here are the rules for surviving this bullshit insanity."

The anticipation of the unknown is what makes life worth living. You hear that jingle? What is it? Is it a dog approaching? Maybe somebody with too many keys? A dog carrying keys? You don't fucking know — and that's what makes it awesome.

Dating is a lot like eating chicken nuggets — except you're the chicken nugget: A bunch of gross shit hidden beneath a golden exterior. And you're going to have to dip around a bit to find somebody with the right sauce to complement your complex, emotionally fried flavor.

I want a woman whose curiosity
is actually quite cautionary. Like,
she's always reading a dark book
or watching a weird documentary —
and, in doing so — she has probably
learned how to hide a body.

The only thing more attractive than confidence is intelligence. Don't believe me? Have a conversation with a confident idiot and let me know how horny it makes you.

Everything has the potential to get better with time. Just because you feel like a piece of shit now doesn't mean you'll never have value — even fossilized dinosaur shit ends up in museums.

Self-betrayal will always be more painful than denial. So, trust your gut when things seem really fucked up.

Fear is like beer: too much
of it and we lose all logic.

The truth will never taste as good as a lie, which is why people get defensive and act offended when you serve it to them (despite it being better for them in the long run). Like a plate of broccoli instead of a piece of cake, people push away what they're not ready to taste.

Filtering yourself to accommodate the feelings of somebody else can lead to a personal feeling of losing yourself. So, unless you enjoy being lost in a jungle of self-doubt — be yourself and let others sort their own shit out.

Life, like sex, feels best when you put some effort into it. You can't just lie there and expect it to get better. Act with purpose, have some passion, put yourself in the right position — then, adjust to make the most of uncomfortable situations.

Let self-respect become your reputation. Be someone who is incredibly hard to fuck with because everybody already knows you don't tolerate any kind of bullshit.

You can only chew your food for so long before it's time to swallow and move on. The same goes for your thinking: stop dwelling on thoughts that drive you fucking nuts — think it, feel it, then move on before it becomes too fucking much.

If you ask me, a mutual sense of humor is the backbone of a bonafide relationship — if you can't laugh together, you don't belong together. Humor bonds are the best because you can roast each other without crying, apologizing, or filing for divorce.

Social media has us following
trends instead of our own personal
vision. How many people do you
think would actually take photos
in front of angel wings on a wall if
social media didn't exist at all?

Heartbreak is a motherfucker.
And, the reason it hurts so much
is because you don't believe you'll
ever find another. But, with pain,
there's also a lot of truth to uncover.
So, allow yourself to feel it —
because you're only a loser if you
don't use it to make you better.

The toilet paper shortage of 2020
is proof that — when faced with
a problem — the majority of
people will focus on shit.

Don't let people park themselves in your life while they figure out their own shit. These are people who waste your time and block others from coming in. Give them a warning — then tell them to get fucking moving before you start issuing tickets for the space they're taking up.

You know what's hot? Somebody who helps you see your blind spots. There's nothing more romantic than a partner who helps you become less idiotic.

Treat everything you read online
like a cheating ex: keep your
fucking guard up.

Time is neither for nor against you; time is created by you. If you want more time to do the things that you want to do, the only person who can make that happen is you. Not your boss, not your boyfriend or girlfriend, and definitely not your cousin. Your power lies within your priorities.

Why dress to impress when you can dress to kill instead? I mean, why dress to get someone's attention when you can dress to teach someone a lesson?

Not everyone will understand
you, but that doesn't mean you're
wrong. Not everyone understands
calculus, physics, or science,
but that doesn't change the
formulas. Instead of thinking you
must change who you are to be
accepted, think to yourself, "Maybe
I'm just fucking complicated."

If you take anything in life as an absolute certainty, you'll find that nearly everything in life becomes contradictory.

You're bored because of your ego. Stop thinking you're too good, too smart, or too cool to be entertained by little things and everything becomes more interesting — especially you.

I don't like people who talk; I like people who do. And, if you spend all your life worrying about what other people are talking about when they talk about you, talking is all you're ever going to fucking do.

Timing is everything. It doesn't matter whether you're here or there if the other person isn't ready to hear or care. Stop wasting your time, breath, and energy on people who aren't prepared to listen, learn, or lay you like you mean something.

Being picky is the best strategy.
Pick your battles, pick your friends,
pick your sexual companions — and
when you lose one (or all) of those
things — pick yourself the fuck up.

Personal growth is uncomfortable for you, but it's also uncomfortable for the people around you — that's why they question, analyze, and disregard your changes. So what? Keep fucking going. If you let others' opinions stop you, you know who's in control of your life? NOT YOU.

Transparency makes everything better: individuals, relationships, politics, clothing — you name it. When there's nothing to hide, there's nothing to fear. And who's afraid of authenticity, honesty, or a little nipple?

If you're truly living your life, mistakes are going to happen — but there's no bigger mistake than a complete lack of action. Hesitation in the name of prevention or protection is often times just an excuse to live your life in a less exciting direction.

Real rebellion comes from not hiding your true feelings. The most rebellious individuals are the most loving because they don't fear shit like heartbreak or rejection. And that's the definition of somebody who truly "doesn't give a fuck" — not some jackass driving a big-ass truck.

If you enjoy talking shit, go meet with a therapist. A complete stranger will point out all of your toxic behaviors, insecurities, and bullshit ways of living —
it's fucking exhilarating.

When you "take a trip" down memory lane, remember, you're there to visit it — not relive it. Look back, but don't lose your current focus. Think, but don't dwell. And, if there's more to leave behind you, tell anyone who needs to hear it, "Go to hell."

You can say all the right things and not get through to someone. You can make all the right moves and not save a relationship. You can hit all the right spots and nobody gets off. Because life isn't about being right; life is about being real. And, real might feel fucking wrong.

A college degree is cool, but
without a moral compass, you're a
piece of shit — an educated piece
of shit, but still a piece of shit.

No matter what you read, see, think, or hear online — remember: There's still a world outside your door and a life outside of your opinion.

All of you who thought you were too smart to ever be fooled by a narcissist, remember when you were obsessed with Joe Exotic?

"Fear of regret" is a real reason why so many people don't work through their bullshit. It's the fear of feeling you should have done something sooner — like you've wasted years — regretting not having made the change a long time ago. And, that fear rationalizes staying the same.

You have to implode the idea of who you think you "should be" if you want to work on becoming who you're meant to be. Forget about blowing up and throwing tantrums — break inward and fix the real fucking problem.

You don't need someone who cooks you breakfast in the morning; you need someone who makes your overall life less boring. Because no amount of pancakes will make up for the fact that you're with somebody who doesn't even make you feel "awake."

Criticism is hard to take when you personally believe it. Love is hard to accept when you personally have to fake it. And, the truth is hard to hear when you personally fear it. In other words, you should focus less on what others are saying — and more on your own personal healing.

Negligence only creates temporary confidence. Ignoring your problems will help you feel better for a moment — but addressing your problems will actually make you a better person. So, what would you rather be: a faker of feelings or a real human being?

Without all of the evidence, you're simply guessing — which is why comparing yourself to others is so fucking depressing. You don't know shit about their lives; you only see what you're shown. And, well, serial killers aren't the only ones hiding shit, trying to remain unknown.

If you say you're going to be somewhere, be there. Consistently canceling plans, or simply not showing up, is childish — and you're getting too old for that shit. Treat your reputation like your skin care routine because flakey is not a good look for anybody.

If you enjoy burning sage to remove the bad energy in a room, you might also want to consider burning some bridges to cleanse your life of the people who are no fucking good for you.

Trust your gut whenever shit
isn't adding up. It doesn't take
a mathematician to know when
2 + 2 = somebody fucking with you.

If you're in a relationship, get a hobby.
Better yet: develop a talent, pursue
a goal, and try something new.
Because you're not on this planet to
make somebody else "your world"
and stop focusing on what you, as an
individual, want to fucking do.

You're not boyfriend or girlfriend material. Seriously, you're not. You're a person; not somebody else's must-have style for a season. So, stop bumming yourself out every time you find out that you're not somebody else's perfect fit — that's dramatic, materialistic bullshit.

To everyone I've upset or offended over
the years with something I've said,
texted, or non-verbally communicated:
Did you take that advice yet?

We live in a time when people will go out of their way and take stupid risks just to get the perfect picture for Instagram, but taking a chance on themselves to live the life they've always pictured is an inconvenience and too much fucking work for them.

Dating is a lot like sailing: it looks
fun, it appears carefree, but it's
pretty fucking complicated and
very few people actually know
what they're doing.

If you don't like what people are
saying about you, don't correct them —
correct your view of them. Stop seeing
others as your source of self-esteem
and you simply won't care what
they're saying or thinking.

It doesn't matter how fucking smart you are, there will always be people who know more than you — you just have to shut up, and open up, long enough to hear their point of view. Speaking without ever listening is like a bunch of dudes sitting in a room talking about menstruating.

It's okay to miss something and still admit that it was wrong for you. A job, a city, a relationship . . . feel free to remember the good times, while giving yourself the freedom to put them behind you in order to focus on a better you.

Bad timing doesn't mean stop trying. Just because a day, a month, or an entire year doesn't align with your desire doesn't mean you should give up and set all your goals on fire. You just need to adjust until things are slightly less fucked up.

If you're waiting for something else
to change before you change yourself,
that's not patience — that's negligence.
Take care of yourself, regardless of
the shit that's going on around you,
because whatever you're waiting for
sure as shit isn't waiting for you.

Silence is for movie theaters, failed comebacks, and awkward first dates. Speaking up is for good sex, social injustice, and changing your fate.

Don't let someone break you
because they don't understand you.
People form opinions based on their
understanding — and most people
don't even fucking understand
themselves — so why would you
take another individual's judgmental
opinion of you as factual?

A private life is a powerful thing
worth protecting. Having one will
keep you safe, sane, and far more
willing to live the life of YOUR
fucking dreams.

When you're watching a movie and there's a scene that you simply cannot fucking stand, do you rewind it to watch it over and over? No. So why do that when thinking about mistakes you've made in life? Move on and keep the story going.

The ideal quarantine companion is someone who respects boundaries, but is open to possibilities. You know, somebody who won't touch your food, but is more than willing to talk about weird shit with you.

It's true, a relationship will require
some sacrifices — but if one of those
sacrifices is your sanity, go take a
look at yourself in the mirror and ask,
"What the fuck is wrong with me?"

Sometimes, you'll cut ties with people
for no reason other than the fact that you
realize you simply don't like the way that
you feel around them (and vice versa).
Neither side has to do something wrong
in order to decide some people just aren't
meant to be in your life for long.

You can't just put a label on something and expect it to grow. A relationship requires cultivation and assurance of connection — it's called romance, you fucking bum.

If she's a fan of Harry Potter, date her. Trust me, she's carrying around enough homemade potions and essential oils to cure pretty much anything except your own stupidity — which is in full effect, by the way, if you let a spiritual witch like her slip away.

You can be both goal-oriented and open to whatever happens. This comes from understanding that not all goals can be controlled, and not all goals are yours to hold. It's not about giving up; it's about not beating yourself up. Because not everything is due to you fucking up.

Without boundaries, your life is anarchy. Whether it involves work, friends, or love — if you don't set and protect your personal space — you'll always feel like something is out of place. And, that's because something is out of place: your fucking priorities.

Sticking to your guns is important — but only if your guns are pointed in the right direction. Otherwise, your stubbornness will actually hinder your progression, making you both the suspect and the hostage in the situation.

Unconditional love is cool, but I want untouchable love. The kind of love that can't be fucked with by others' opinions, lies, or influence. A love that is rooted in trust and strengthened by a sense of humor. Instead of getting upset, you simply laugh at dumb shit together.

A connection can only be as strong
as your communication. If you don't
talk about what's really going on, you
sabotage your potential bond.

Feeling lost is not an excuse to fuck your life up. If you were stranded in the middle of the ocean, would you sink your fucking boat just because you're unsure of your destination?

At some point in your life, you're going to want to give up — on a dream, a project, or maybe even a person. But, you won't. Then, another point in your life will come when you'll look back and see how wrong your life would be had you been done. And, that feeling is why we try.

Mental shifts are more important than physical trips. You can move, travel, and surround yourself with new people, but — without a new state of mind — you'll continue chasing something that's impossible to physically find.

The people who don't know you will
be the first to criticize you because
those who know nothing have
opinions about everything.

Don't mistake acknowledgment for engagement. Acknowledgment is simply somebody validating that you're there, whereas engagement comes from someone who actually cares. In other words, if your efforts aren't met with action, it's time you, or somebody else, started packing.

The best girlfriends are both independent and intentional. Like, she doesn't need your opinion, but if she asks for it, it's because she's planning something — and that shit is going to fucking happen. (Bonus points if what is about to happen doesn't end in a murder investigation.)

If you have a problem with someone on social media, unfollow them. If you're afraid to unfollow them because of their reaction, guess what? That's still only your problem.

As someone who deals with it, I'll say from experience: Procrastination is a mental prison for anyone with depression. Putting off work and responsibility feeds shame and insecurity — making it hard to enjoy damn near everything. Simply getting shit done has helped me immensely.

Your reputation is what the majority of people think of you — not what everybody thinks of you. A variety of opinions means you're a good, authentic, not trying-too-hard kind of human. If everyone has the same opinion of you, you're either a people-pleaser or a fucking asshole.

Acknowledging a fucked-up situation
doesn't negate personal responsibility
or action. The world feeds off of fear
and negativity — which can affect how
you feel — but it's up to you to decide
if you selectively heal, just deal, or
take the fucking wheel.

Not all loss is a loss; sometimes, you need a loss to become a boss. Lose the parts of your lifestyle that no longer serve you, lose the people in your life who no longer support you, and definitely lose whatever fucking attitude has you believing the world owes you.

Emotional intelligence is the
ultimate form of independence. Sure,
having money, traveling, and being
mysteriously unavailable all the time
feels like freedom — but you'll still
be tied down if you can't navigate
others' emotions and effectively
communicate your own.

Talk, argue, and get to the bottom of issues;
find common ground when shit feels
upside down. More personal understanding,
less taking things personally. More
obsession with connection, less addiction
to attention. More "I'm listening," less
"I'm offended, so now you're canceled."

The cool thing about life is that you don't have to follow instructions on how to live it if you don't want to. Like building something from IKEA, you can learn as you go. Sure, your version might not resemble the pictures — but, fuck it, at least your version has character.

Maybe the grass looks greener because you're looking at your phone instead of watching where you're going. And, you're going to step in shit if you don't learn to focus your attention on your own direction.

You need a generous dealer. Not someone who gives you free drugs and shit, but someone who gives you a dose of reality when you need to hear it. Sure, drugs can be fun — especially when you're not paying for them — but great advice will fuck you up in ways that last much longer.

A title does not define you. Boyfriend, girlfriend, fuck-buddy, slam-piece, etc. — these are roles that you play in somebody else's life — not words that establish the purpose of your life. You're an individual. And, you need a goal that's exclusive of your relationship role.

Crazy shit happens when you begin
to surround yourself with like-minded
individuals: Your goals feel attainable,
your conversations become more
meaningful, and you can actually find
a bar or a restaurant to go to on a
Friday night that's fucking agreeable.

Forget about breaking down someone's walls; build a door that only you can access. As long as you can get in, it's okay for someone you're with to still be guarded. Just make sure you close the door behind you — THE A/C IS ON. How else do you think their heart stays so cold?

The holy grail of dating is finding an individual who's intellectual, thoughtful, comical, and unusual. You know, somebody who's smart with a good heart, a respect for the fact that sarcasm is an art, and a willingness to do weird shit with your private parts.

Life is all about knowing when to spit
and when to swallow. Spit it out; some
things need to be said. Swallow your
pride; asking for help can get you ahead.
And, well, very few people actually
deserve your freak moves in bed.

Sexual kinks are perfectly normal
and healthy. Life's too short to not
free your wild side from time to time.
Hell, even Rapunzel wasn't freed until
some guy pulled her hair correctly.

"Making the first move" applies to more than dating. You can't always wait for others to offer — ask for that promotion, speak up if you have a question, stand in the right place to get the bartender's attention — get the money, answers, and buzz you fucking desire and deserve.

When you start to do something different or new, you'll likely receive one of three responses: "Good luck" (passive support), "You suck" (active resistance), or "What the fuck?" (general ignorance) — it's all worthless feedback. All that really matters is having your own back.

You cannot be anything you want to be in life, but you can be REALLY FUCKING GREAT at something. Uncover your natural talent, learn a new skill — keep fucking failing until you find a path worth pursuing. And, if you're only good at failing, start a podcast or something.

Live each day without fear: get
dressed without using a mirror.

During summer, both sarcasm
and sunscreen need to be applied
regularly. Because thick skin is just
as important as beautiful skin. So, do
your friends a favor: help them with
the hard-to-reach spots — but also
hit them with plenty of that because-
we're-friends style of shit talk.

Stop being so fucking hard on
yourself. If you're paying the rent,
going out each weekend, and buying
fruit that's already sliced — you're
fucking thriving. Relax and enjoy your
apples, you boujee asshole.

Never argue with your girlfriend while she's wearing a face mask; YOU WILL LOSE. For starters, she's relaxing, who are you to fuck that up? Secondly, with that mask on, she's basically a luchador — and she's ready to emotionally elbow drop your ass.

Fun Fact: Move the C, replace the E, and the word "office" becomes the word "coffin." Anyway, have fun at work today.

Dumbing yourself down to make others comfortable is like a lion walking into a room and acting like a kitten: Sure, it might seem cute, but cute didn't earn lions the title of "Kings and Queens of the Fucking Jungle."

No people-pleaser has ever become a
respected leader. Sure, one might find
a way to the top, but even a pigeon can
land on a high ledge — still a flying
fucking rat though.

Someday, you're going to wake up and say, "Holy fuck, this is my life." So, do whatever you can today, tomorrow, and the next to ensure that the "fuck" you say on that day is being used in a positive fucking way.

I want a girl who's responsive, but slightly overreactive. Like, she always answers your texts in timely fashion — but if you ignore hers for too long — it's possible her next move will be considered "a crime of passion."

The cool thing about being wrong is that admitting it doesn't make you any more wrong — it actually helps you learn and move on. I have a feeling a lot of people will need this mindset after reading this book.

The way I see it, the guy should ALWAYS pay for the first date, just to even things out. Have you been inside a Sephora? An eye shadow palette is about 45 bucks — that's five times the price of mozzarella sticks.

You don't have to be perfect to
have a positive impact. Effecting
change requires the discovery and
acknowledgment of common ground.
And, the one thing we all have in
common: We're all a little fucked up.

Looks fade and money goes, but humor is everlasting. Seek those who match your wit, appreciate your dark shit (you know you're sick), and have the ability to laugh with you through the worst of it. A boring life simply means you've chosen to fill it with boring people.

Remember that show "My Strange Addiction" with people addicted to weird shit like eating couch cushions and dressing up in lizard costumes? That was sweet. Now everyone's addicted to dumb shit like avocado toast and staring at their phone.

Don't date someone in hopes of changing them; you cannot "design" the perfect human. You know who tried this? Dr. Frankenstein. You know what he ended up with? A fucking monster.

I want a woman with the attitude of a clown, but the character worthy of a crown. Like, she doesn't take herself too seriously, but — if you cross her — her reaction will go down in the pages of fucking history.

You don't like people forcing their opinions on you, so why do you allow them to force their emotions and behavior? Psychological projection is so fucking common these days — but, you don't have to be mad, sad, or stupid just because the majority of your social media feed is.

Did you know horned lizards squirt blood from their eyes when they feel threatened? Imagine crying tears of blood whenever something was bothering you — your boss would have no choice other than to constantly promote you because they'd be so deathly afraid of your sad demon ass.

Stop reliving the mistakes of your past and focus on the moments of today. Replaying a situation over and over again in your head is not a productive way to live — that's a fucking Boomerang and it belongs on your annoying friend's Instagram.

Dating apps are designed to make
you desperate by overwhelming
you with options that aren't actually
options because everyone begins to
view everyone else as an optional
commodity rather than a potential
connection, causing you to feel like shit
about yourself and your situation.

"Don't ask questions you don't want to know the answer to" is terrible advice; that's a sheltered way to live your life. Fuck that, ask all of the questions — just don't let all of the answers affect you. (Because a lot of answers will be dumb, wrong, or not reflective of you.)

Just because somebody is always there doesn't mean they actually care. Learn to differentiate between loyalty and leeching. Some people are truly standing by your side; others are just sticking around for a free ride.

Remove yourself — from situations, relationships, and shit that simply doesn't make sense. You can't begin to put your life together until you stop putting your time and energy into people, projects, and private parts that don't really matter.

Anybody can have sex — find somebody
who can have a conversation. Because
it's all fun and foreplay until you want
to talk about something other than,
"How was your day?"

Vulnerability is a venereal disease. Don't hide. Don't use protection. Pass that shit on. Because the more it spreads from person to person, the less alone everybody feels. Share your feelings and fucking heal.

You're only as boring as you allow yourself to be. Tortillas look plain as fuck — but they can become all sorts of stuff — chips, burritos, tacos, layers, shells, etc. So, if you're feeling lame, you're just not being creative enough.

Sadly, a lot of people don't know
how to think for themselves
because they haven't made a
serious decision without social
media input since 2007.

In life, you find what you're looking for. If you're looking for a reason to dislike someone, that's easily done. If you're looking for reasons to be happy, you'll find plenty. And, if you're looking for a reason to be offended or upset, allow me to introduce you to the Internet.

Not putting your past behind you is the same as allowing your shadow to define you. Both are nonexistent versions of yourself: Don't dwell on old mistakes — you're no longer that person at all. Don't let your shadow fool you — you're not that fucking tall.

In bee society, the queen is routinely killed off using the "cuddle death" method. Basically, worker bees pile around her until she dies from overheating; she's then replaced by a younger female. All I'm saying is, cuddling after sex is a trap. Resist. Remain the fucking queen.

An obsession with perfection
will prevent you from having real
connection. To always have the
perfect answer, action, and attitude —
you can't be yourself. And, you need
to be yourself so you can fuck up.
Then, learn and grow. THAT will bring
you closer than any perfect answer.

EVERYTHING you do in life should fuel your dream. Where you live, what you eat, who you fuck — these choices will either inspire your creativity, sustain your energy, or text you so fucking often that both your patience and data plan become nonexistent. Choose wisely.

If you ask me, the best traits you can have in life are experience and independence. Sure, being nice and attractive also have a place — but I've never seen anyone open a stubborn jar with kind words or their face.

Be your own best friend. Laugh at your own jokes. Hype yourself up in the mirror. Plan a night out for yourself. Cut yourself off when you've clearly had too many (or buy another shot — depends which kind of best friend you're trying to be).

Here's an idea: Instead of sending
lonely, late-night texts to someone
who's probably going to ignore you
anyway, read a book — try using
your imagination for something
other than your dating life.

Hell is knowing what you want, but not having it at the moment. So, if your life feels like Hell right now — at least you have a vision of something better. The dog will come back in the room, your food will be delivered soon, and being single doesn't mean you're fucking doomed.

When you act with entitlement, you deserve disappointment. Entitlement is expecting something, for yourself, that can only be fulfilled by somebody else. That's a powerless position to put yourself in. And, well, that might explain why you're always fucking crying.

I'm all for saving the trees and
the polar bears, but can we also
concentrate on saving our collective
sense of humor? Temperatures and
sensitivity levels are on the rise, and
if these trends continue, the next
generation will be living in a barren,
butthurt wasteland.

A shelter can protect you from the storm, but it can also prevent you from seeing the sun. Meaning, it's okay to find safety in stability, but don't get so fucking comfortable that you lose sight of your own ability.

If you're in a relationship, it's normal to still find other people attractive — art exists in many forms. However, if you're a decent human, act like you're in a museum: look and appreciate, then go touch, fuck, and adjust something at home.

Your ego is an obstacle that must be overcome if you have any desire to grow and move on. It's a wall that prevents learning, and an excuse to ignore thoughts worth hearing. So, either get the fuck over yourself, or get comfortable with a stubborn and stupid version of yourself.

The more you focus on missing out on something, the more you miss out on simply living. Instead of creating memories, you create doubt and uncertainty. You question (or regret) most of your decisions, which, over time, makes you an increasingly negative and boring person.

Convenience isn't something you're obligated to offer to anyone. When it comes to your time, nobody should feel like they're buying that shit on Amazon. Set whatever hours, parameters, and emotional guards you find necessary to your energy and sanity.

Too many of us are seeking someone
or something that looks good on us,
as opposed to finding individuals
and interests that are good for us. It
doesn't matter who you're dating or
what you're wearing — you'll never
be happy — if all you care about is
how many people are staring.

The assumptions you make influence the actions you put into play. So, unless you're trying to play fucking dumb, it's best you don't make assumptions about anyone.

Don't let the words that come out of others' mouths deter you from figuring your shit out. If you're in the process of changing for the better, anyone who questions that is not a friend — they're a fucker.

I mean, sure, sex is great — but have you ever layered your outfit perfectly for the weather? Not too hot, not too cold, just the blissful feeling of knowing that, even though the rest of your life is a fucking mess, you absolutely nailed getting dressed?

Approach every Monday like a
bear emerging from hibernation:
fierce, hungry, and barely holding
it together. (The last part simply
means you had a good weekend.)

Women like men who make plans,
commit to those plans, and still
have a few surprises left in them.
This is why your girlfriend is
obsessed with serial killers.

You know when something smells so bad that you have to take a second (or even third) sniff just to confirm how truly awful it is? Yeah, I think that's the same reason people get back with a shitty ex.

I'm pretty sure aliens haven't contacted Earth for the same reason you no longer talk to the friends you had in high school: They've moved on to more rewarding conversations.

Just because it's comfortable doesn't mean it's right for you. This is not about fashion — but rather, your life, your work, your relationships — don't mistake a comfortable fit for the best you can fucking get.

Not everybody who disagrees with you is a "hater." Learn to differentiate between people who are just talking shit about you and people who actually know some shit that can help you.

Be selective with your favors and
the messes you choose to clean;
there are people who will view you
as more of a paper towel than a
human being: Good for one use,
then discarded with the garbage.

Who you are when you're alone is who you should strive to become when you're not at home. That level of comfort requires confidence. And, that's the type of confidence that will take you places — places that are cooler than your couch.

The fact that some people go to a restaurant and treat the staff like shit is fucking ridiculous. You CHOSE to go out to eat. If you feel the need to be rude while you're waiting for your food — stay the fuck home and yell at your microwave.

Be hard on yourself, but never for the actions of somebody else. Don't beat yourself up or feel dumb because you decided to trust or rely on someone — move on — their shit does not make you an idiot (unless you decide not to learn anything from it).

There's no such thing as a "failed" relationship; that's a bullshit way of grading the complexity of human connection. A break-up, a divorce, or even a mysterious disappearance is not a failure — it's a positive decision to find better, feel better, or take a fucking vacation.

Before you commit to dating someone, make sure they don't have prior commitments that will interfere with your fun. Like a jogging routine, a strange way of eating, or somebody else they're already fucking.

A strong dislike for something can
actually make you a better person.
For example: I hate people who lie;
therefore, I call them out on their bullshit
consistently for the benefit of society.

People place blame wherever they place power, which is why blaming others is one of the weakest things you can do; you're giving power to other people — when you should be giving power to your fucking self.

Save your attention for people who
support your progression. If they
don't feed your mind, fuck you right,
or fuel your fire — don't let them
waste your time, ruin your night,
or fuck up your eyeliner.

Ask anyone what they'd do with a time machine and most people will say they'd use it to go back in time to change something. And THAT is the problem with the outlook of too many people: they focus on changing past mistakes instead of looking ahead to create their future.

Spend time alone to learn more about yourself; some of your life's most important questions can only be answered correctly when you're away from everybody: Who are you, really? Where do you want to be in five years? Why are you so stressed? What the fuck is that smell? And so on.

My kink is making people think. Sure, talking dirty is great in the bedroom, but the real fun begins when you find someone who will talk about aliens, history, and conspiracy theories with you.

When somebody tells you that you can't
do something, don't use it as a chance
to prove them wrong, use it as a chance
to get gone. If you remain surrounded by
people who fucking suck, you're going to
have a hell of a time becoming unstuck.

Stop worrying about what others are thinking — start worrying about the time you're wasting. Less "What should I say?" and more "Hey, I like your face." Less "I don't know," and more "Fuck it, I'm getting old." Less "I wonder what it feels like?" and more "Holy shit, this tickles."

Think about this: In a parallel universe, there's an alternate version of yourself, making all of the right choices and doing everything according to plan. And, their life is fucking boring; they long for an adventure because life is predictable and they've never been hungover.

Social media is the ball pit of human existence: On the surface, everyone's life seems colorful, bouncy, and fun — but at the bottom of every ball pit — there's childhood trauma, crusty-ass socks, and the kind of shit that can only be cured with a penicillin shot.

There's a time and place for everything, but the time to send a dick pic is never and the place to put your phone is back in your fucking pocket. (Feel free to choose the pocket — your cargo shorts have 17 of them.)

Don't accept present frustrations as permanent situations. If you don't like something, change it. Leave your boring-ass hometown, lose the friends who weigh you down, and, if somebody is sleeping around — by all means — dump that fucking clown.

No matter how divided the world becomes, we remain united in the sense that we will all die. And, while alive, we're all seeking the same things in life: snacks, satisfaction, and serenity — bonus if you find someone who brings you all three when it's time to get fucking dirty.

I like people who are deliberate; I
like people who do shit on fucking
purpose. I'm all for winging it to keep
things weird and unpredictable, but
somebody who thinks, fucks, and lives
with a plan is fucking irresistible.

Just because you're used to
something doesn't mean that it's no
longer bad for you; you can build up
a tolerance to poison just as easily
as you can a terrible-ass person.
Adapting to somebody's toxicity is
a choice — not a requirement.

Success requires scrubbing. Your friendships, your mindset, your lifestyle, your surroundings — to get to where you really want to be in life — you will need to declutter regularly. I mean, your juice cleanse is cool, but what you really need are friends who aren't fucking tools.

Your ego is a storm at sea, and it will drown you if you don't seek the safety of humility. It doesn't matter how experienced or intelligent you are, if you're cocky, you're traveling through life on a fucking dinghy.

Your sanity should be at the top of your dating priorities. If somebody gets on your fucking nerves, why would you ever allow them to get in your pants?

When you worry more about what others think instead of what you feel, your life becomes a reflection of their opinions instead of a life of authentic actions. This is like allowing somebody else to order for you at a restaurant, even though you already know what you want.

Fear is looking at a river and imagining how it feels to drown. Love is looking at the same river and picturing a way to cross it. So, in life, you can either practice holding your breath — or you can stop acting like a little bitch and start building a bridge.

Trust your gut; it's telling you things
that you need to hear, even though the
messages might not appear very clear.
For example: Maybe your stomach
always hurting has nothing to do with
eating junk food and everything to do
with acting like a damn fool.

One of the most humbling talks
that you can have with yourself
is considering the possibility that
the people you believe you have
outgrown may have actually
outgrown you.

The words "politician" and "magician" have the same ending because they have the same end goal: to distract you with one thing while they make something else disappear.

Looking is not learning just as a question is not the answer — they're both starting points. And, unless you do the work that follows, you'll never complete the process. This is especially true with personal growth; you can't just look in the mirror and ask, "Why am I like this?"

Imagine if you took your own
advice as seriously as you take other
people's opinions. In other words,
imagine getting shit done instead of
worrying about impressing someone.
That's fucking freedom.

Occasionally, in order to set yourself
free, you must upset somebody.
Not everyone will understand your
reasons, support your actions, or
agree with your opinions — but part
of being free is learning to say and
believe, "This is me. And, I won't
change simply because you disagree."

Don't let setbacks affect your self-worth. If you base your self-esteem on the distance you are from achieving your dreams, your life is going to be a fucking nightmare. Because you'll value yourself based on your current place in life — instead of just being yourself at all times.

There's no equation to get life right. You have to try, start over, fuck up, evolve, and keep going. Sure, this takes time and will undoubtedly come with pain — but, if life were a math problem — everybody's life would be the same. Plus, what kind of sick fuck likes math anyway?

With four-letter words, we can offend others; with shorter words, we can offend ourselves. When you choose to say "yes" or "no" to an experience, you choose to either commit or protect your energy. (And just so you know, "fuck that shit" is also an appropriate way of saying no.)

Ladies, don't ever be afraid to make the first move. Any guy who is turned off by your confidence is probably turned off by other attractive things — like kissing with tongues and telling the truth.

Unfinished business has no fucking
business in your life. Whether it's work, love,
or dinner — if you truly care — go all in and
put it all out there. Leave no leftovers. Give
it your all and at least you know that your
commitment will never be at fault.

Do what you gotta do to get through the shit you're going through. If you want to read, do that. If you want to binge-watch garbage reality TV, do that (but don't talk to me about it). Whatever you do, just don't tell yourself that you have to do what everybody else expects you to do.

Living vicariously through other people's social media posts is the same as watching porn: it's a hell of a lot more fun to actually do it. So, stop jerking off to someone else's lifestyle and start showing up for your own fucking life.

Whenever you fuck something up,
apologize to yourself the same way
you would apologize to somebody
else. If you're the kind of person
who never apologizes to anyone —
congratulations, you're an asshole.

A best friend should be both
ruthlessly loyal and loyal enough
to be ruthless. In other words, they
should always have your back — but
still call you out on the dumb shit
that's holding you back.

Too many people refer to
themselves as a "control freak" like
it's an endearing little quirk. It's not.
It means you're a pain in the ass
who can't adapt to change.

Love is a drug — and you have to get
high on your own supply. Because
if you're not personally feeling what
you're dealing, how can you expect
another person to feel comfortable
revealing what they're feeling?

The older I get, the more patience
I have for individuals who are just
being themselves — and the less
patience I have for people who are
trying so fucking hard to be just
like everyone else.

If there's one thing I know for certain about life: There's no such thing as "finally." There's no "Finally, I can be happy," "Finally, I won't stress," or "Finally, I can enjoy this" — there will always be something (or someone) to test you, tempt you, or take fries from you.

In a relationship, there's a significant difference between taking turns and keeping score: When you take turns, you're sharing a burden. When you keep score, you're playing games.

Fear is relatable, which makes it
easy to spread. Ask yourself: Am I
being told the truth, or is somebody
just fucking with my head?

If you disagree with someone, that's fucking awesome — disagreements create movements. But, be mature with your argument . . . complaining will never be convincing.

You know the feeling you get when you find a healthy alternative that you like even more than the junk food you were eating before? Relationships work the same way: Don't get so addicted to toxic shit that you forget there are better, healthier, far fucking tastier options out there.

There's a serious difference between self-discipline and disciplining yourself — keeping yourself motivated to get shit done won't happen if you talk more shit to yourself than anyone.

Self-care is important, but caring about other people keeps you from becoming a self-centered asshole.

In life, nothing is controllable — except your own behavior. So, do yourself a favor, and prepare for the future, by deciding to be less of a whiner and more of a "whatever the fuck happens, I got this" kind of thinker.

Learning how you learn best might be the best thing you ever learn. Some learn by reading, others learn by listening, and a lot of us learn the hard way. But, make no mistake, if you know better and choose not to do better, that's not "the hard way" — that's just being a dumbass.

I want a girl whose remarks are bold, but whose heart is gold. Like, she's not afraid to talk some shit, but she'd also save a puppy from the street despite the fear of getting hit.

If we replaced cancel culture with critical thinking, we'd have empathetic conversations instead of emotional reactions. And, by talking, we learn to separate honest mistakes from actual hate.

When the truth slaps you in the face,
take it and listen. Don't pretend like it
didn't happen. Because each reminder
after that is going to make it harder and
harder to separate fiction from fact.

The ideal relationship is one where you can be yourself, but still learn about yourself. Speak your mind, but still be challenged sometimes. Be independent, but still know you have a support system. Feel comfortable, but still try new shit that tickles and scares you a little.

Dating is like a dressing room: Some people are looking for comfort, others are just concerned with how it looks — but in the end — if it doesn't fit, fucks your credit, or makes you self-conscious, it's not fucking worth it.

Playing the victim becomes addictive because it focuses solely on YOUR pain and perspective. And, sometimes, in order to get over something — you have to first get over yourself.

I want to be around people who are open-minded, but not easily offended. You know, people who appreciate differences — enough to understand that my sense of humor is different/darker/better than theirs.

I fucking love seeing people in love.
I used to be so opposed to public
displays of affection. Now, it's like,
"Hey, life is fucking hard. If you
find someone who makes it more
enjoyable, do your thing — just keep
your pants on, your hands visible,
and the slurping inaudible."

I'd much rather live a life of going
"all in" than live a life acting
"too cool" to give a fuck about
someone or something.

Personal growth is not perfectly gained. You're going to have moments of weakness, you're going to wonder if you've regressed, and sometimes you're going to feel like a fucking mess — but it's called "growth" for a reason — and your old patterns are your growing pains.

Stop knocking people who are obsessed with pumpkin spice. Sure, it's fucking gross, but so is using Tinder to keep your dating life afloat. Moral of the story: Everybody has their own way of clinging to hope — let them have it.

A fact is information minus emotion.
An opinion is information plus
experience. Ignorance is an opinion
lacking information. And, stupidity
is an opinion that ignores a fact.

Dating Tip: Personal growth is the new six-pack. Because nobody is going to give a fuck about your abs if all you do is bring up problems from your past.

Don't let anyone make you feel weak because you're feeling broken. At some point, everybody cracks, breaks, and falls apart — but not everybody has the strength to put it back together. And, the people who don't heal just want you to feel how they feel: shitty.

I don't understand how people lose interest in learning new things. You mean to tell me you're at a point in your life where you're just like, "Fuck it, I know enough"? How is that even possible? Are you dead, dumb, or just lazy?

I'm all for changing your opinion when presented with new information. But, allowing your opinion to be changed by popularity alone means you didn't have an opinion to begin with — you were simply seeking validation from the "cool kids."

There's no progression in a purely
physical connection. If they don't also
support your mental health, you're
never going to become your best self.
In other words, wait for someone who
can both fuck your brains out AND
help you figure your shit out.

The fake arguments you practice (and hopefully win) in the shower reveal actual fears and insecurities. So, pay attention to what you're saying and thinking because there's no winning if you don't figure out why the hell you're feeling that way in the first place.

If you feel the need to always defend yourself, take it as a sign that it's time to distance yourself. Friendships, relationships, and even "What is this?"-ships are built on connection, not retaliation. Anything worth sticking around for won't require you to always go to war.

Turns out, the old-age filters are just warnings to let you know that you're going to be in the same place in life when you're 85 if you don't get off your phone, stop taking selfies, and go do something with your fucking life.

Using the word "need" does not equal "needy." It's okay (in fact, it's fucking healthy) to know what you NEED in a partner. Stating what you require to feel secure, supported, and engaged in a relationship has nothing to do with "needing a person" and/or losing your independence.

The adult version of trick-or-treating is posting your costume on Instagram for comments instead of going door to door for candy. It's basically the same thing; you know, except, as adults, we like to destroy our mental health in addition to our physical health.

Cuddle season, cuffing season, blah, blah, blah — call it what it really is: The Monster Months. This is the time of year when you either hook up with a monster, dress up as a monster, or give up and reveal the monster you really are.

HALLOWEEN

Dudes, get into the Halloween spirit. If you're going to send a dick pic, send a picture of your empty hand instead. Tell her you're holding a ghost dick (ooh, so spooky). In fact, use this technique all year long — nobody wants to fucking see your weird goblin wiener anyway.

The ideal relationship should be with someone who's supportive, but not indulgent. Like, they'll cheer you on while you chase your dreams, but they'll also give you a reality check when shit is clearly not happening.

Don't wait for spring to do your cleaning.
If there's something/someone that needs
to go, do it now. Holding on to things that
no longer have a place in your life isn't
"saving" — it's hoarding. And, hoarding
is fucking gross; it prevents you from
having space for something else.

Expectations set the tone of every situation. And, if you choose to set yours correctly, or remove them entirely, you can change your life's story. Because when we are honest with ourselves, or somebody else, we no longer create villains in scenarios that have no need for a hero.

Be an all-until-nothing kind of person.
Meaning, give it your all until you
know there's nothing because, trust
me, half-assing something you care
about is far worse than losing.

There's a big difference between being a bully and being someone who doesn't stand for bullshit. The main difference being this: If you're a bully, you're part of the bullshit.

You will never encounter anything as fiercely defensive as a mama bear protecting her cubs, a rattlesnake having a bad day, or a girlfriend about to get tickled. In those moments, any of these creatures will not hesitate to end your life.

Every relationship will face a moment meant to fucking break you. And your time together will either end or you'll become stronger than you ever imagined. Now, if you have to question whether or not that moment has happened, it hasn't. So, sit back, the real shit has yet to hit.

Obsessing over the past will never bring it back — which is fucking great. Because "past you" made a lot of dumb decisions, right? And, you know what else is dumb? Thinking about your past decisions instead of focusing on your current direction.

Whenever you're feeling powerless —
like your decisions don't really matter —
think about this: If you're single, your
decisions can fuck up your life. If you're
in a relationship, your decisions can fuck
up somebody else. If you have kids, your
decisions can fuck up generations.

If you don't believe you'll make it
through a break-up, you should
break up. Because you're in an
unhealthy relationship and no one
should be that dependent on another
person. Trust me, you'll live —
you beautiful, dramatic idiot.

Fuck your diet. Try eliminating all the unhealthy relationships from your life instead. Because it doesn't matter how good you look in a bathing suit if you have jealous friends willing to backstab you.

Just a reminder: Authenticity can coexist with mystery; you don't owe everyone an explanation. Sometimes, being your true self means keeping some things to yourself — like your opinion, for example.

Pay attention to all of your
"freethinker" friends who are actually
the quickest to assume whatever
mindset is currently trending.

After 2020, you can't seriously date anyone without factoring in the very fucking real possibility of being quarantined with them for a couple of months — no work, no nights with friends, no trips to keep things interesting . . . Just you, and their personality.

Time in quarantine must be tough for people who live for meaningless gossip. When social interaction hits an all-time low, a lot of people are forced to talk about their own lives and goals — realizing they have neither.

When we don't listen, life will happily give us a much-needed lesson — multiple times even. So, be a good student the first time and life won't interrupt as many of your good times.

Billionaires are fucking boring. Your mega mansions with all-white furniture make me sick. How could you have that kind of money and not live in a haunted castle with a moat, hedges shaped like animals, and a groundskeeper with a questionable past?

Resistance to learning is acceptance of a problem returning. You can never know too much, but you can absolutely know too little. Nothing you learn is useless, but you can easily waste something useful. And, you can't be better/smarter tomorrow if you refuse to learn from today.

If you don't value your reputation, don't expect anyone to validate your contributions; you show people how seriously to take you by how seriously you take yourself. And, unless you want your life to be a joke, you occasionally need to start a fire when somebody is blowing smoke.

A reaction without comprehension is just an excuse to be offended. And, it's a major problem (particularly, on social media) because too many people have made a habit of seeing and immediately commenting, rather than reading and actually comprehending.

People change, feelings fade, and only closed-minded individuals remain the same forever. In other words, instead of being too quick to judge someone's past behavior, remember the fact that you, yourself, were once somebody you'd consider wrong, naive, or different altogether.

All that you truly own in life are your
emotions. Everything else either
contributes to or distracts from what you
are feeling and where you are going. So,
pay attention to how shit makes you feel.
Then, avoid the undesirable shit like
you would a Mario Kart banana peel.

Realize the importance of living in
the moment before you find yourself
remembering the past. Seriously, if you
woke up today feeling or looking semi-
decent — enjoy it — because you don't
know how long that shit will last.

THANKSGIVING

I like people who decorate early for
Christmas because they live life on
their own time. Pancakes at 10pm? Hell
yeah. A beer for breakfast? Absolutely.
Two reindeer humping in the front yard
a week before Thanksgiving?
Happy fucking Holidays.

Society has you fooled into believing you have to "accept" criticism in order to be successful. You don't. You don't have to accept shit. But, you do have to learn to organize it — separate feedback that's worth a damn from those who just criticize whatever they don't understand.

FOMO is a form of self-betrayal
because it denies the importance of
your own life. Don't turn your back
on your own reality just because
you saw some fake-ass influencer
kicking back on a beach in Italy.

Why is it that the people who claim they "don't have time for bullshit" always seem to be the ones most intent on spreading it?

Nobody wants to be a nobody, but not everybody is willing to be somebody. Because being somebody requires you to do things that not everybody is willing to do. Like, think for yourself, speak up when you disagree with something, and accept that the world truly owes you nothing.

If you're flavorful, rejection is fucking inevitable. A strong personality is an acquired taste; just because one person thinks your flavor is shit doesn't mean another won't think you're fucking delicious.

Count all the times in a typical week
that you do (or don't do) something
solely because you're worried about
what somebody might think of you if
you did otherwise — that's how many
times each week you are living a lie.

Forget about fitting in, focus on figuring yourself out. If you want to be a cool fucking human, develop a willingness to learn, grow, and be honest with yourself and others. Because that's the shit that really matters if you're trying to be someone who's remembered.

You can't describe yourself as "competitive" and then be against equal rights. If you were truly such a great competitor, that shit wouldn't matter. The only reason anyone is against racial or gender equality is because they know — without an advantage — they're a fucking loser.

People talk shit when you have something they're trying to get. Maybe it's success, maybe it's attention, maybe it's a person — the ones who feel the need to always say something bad are often times just mad that they don't have what you have.

If you want to be liked, make others comfortable. If you want to live your best life, do things that are uncomfortable. The choice is yours — but don't live your life as a sofa for so fucking long that you fail to realize when it's time to stand up for yourself and move on.

People become dumb when they're too horny and obsessive, just like people become dumb when they're too judgy and offended — oddly enough, both types of people just need to get fucking laid.

Don't waste your life trying to
impress people only to realize the
people you are trying to impress are
trying to impress you by not acting
too impressed by what you do.

Instead of trying to be the hottest person in the room, try being the most honest person that people know. Trust me, you have a better chance at it. Not to mention, a truthful character will actually make you hotter.

When unexpected shit happens, you have two choices: flow with it or fight with it. Pick your fights carefully though because the universe isn't in a hurry — it has nothing but energy and time. Don't wait 'til you're about to die to learn what you could've learned while fully alive.

As humans, we hate uncertainty, but we love surprises. We thrive on habit, but dislike the same old bullshit. We know what's good for us, but we choose what fucks with us. And, this is why sex, religion, and elections will always be confusing.

You can't pick and choose facts
like pizza toppings. Ignoring truths
because you don't like how they taste
is the reason why so many people
remain stuck in place. If you want to
grow, you'd better learn to swallow.

There will come a time in your life when you will doubt nearly fucking everything you're about. Maybe it's today, maybe it's tomorrow, or maybe it's a year from now — whenever it is — remember, there are people dumber than you living the life you want to live.

A lot of people don't actually want to change, they want to complain. This is why you hear so many people talk, yet remain exactly the same. Like that friend who keeps saying they're going to leave your hometown, but every time you visit, there they are, still hanging around.

There's power in being alone. And, once you get over the initial discomfort, there's an entirely new world to uncover — a world full of self-reliance, newfound confidence, and snacking as loud as you fucking want during a movie without judgment or consequence.

Don't let others force-feed you their emotions. A lot of people online want you to eat shit just because they're currently eating shit. Fuck that. If you don't like it, you don't have to try it — stay on an emotional diet.

Size matters. Support small business this holiday season. And, don't act like small isn't already your thing — just look at your dog, your purse, and your boyfriend.

It's okay to feel things; in fact, it's necessary. Everyone these days is so afraid of "catching feelings" that they inadvertently close off their natural instincts and better fucking judgment, which will actually leave you feeling the worst feeling of all: feeling fucking dumb.

The gift and the curse of your imagination is that it's not constrained by the truth of any situation. You can use it to either stress yourself out or figure your shit out. The only difference is the direction you allow your imagination to go.

If you insist on being perfect (which will never fucking happen), try being perfect in your efforts — not perfect in the effects that you have on others. Because even your best intentions will miss others' expectations.

Fibonacci sequences are
mathematical patterns of repetition
that can often be seen in nature.
Likewise, some dudes' behavior is
perfectly predictable because being
a fuckboy is simply in their nature.

Protected sanity is more important than protected sex. I don't care how good somebody fucks, it's not worth it if they make you feel like you suck. Nobody rides dick or squishes lips so fucking well that it justifies going through emotional hell.

Confirmation bias is dangerous
because it makes you believe that your
opinion is the center of everything.
But, it's not. Your opinion is simply the
closest YOU have come to the truth.
And, the truth cannot be found if you
continue to believe, "Everything is
meant to support me."

Remember when everybody was panic-buying dumb shit like toilet paper because they were afraid of an apocalypse? Well, do you want to know what's equally fucking ridiculous? Panic-dating any dumbass who gives you attention because you're afraid of being alone.

Your life is like a Christmas cookie:
Decorate it however the fuck you
want. The taste, the texture, the
toppings — it's all up to you. And, if
somebody doesn't like your cookie,
that's fine; save it for someone
who wants to eat it.

Before you build a life together, build a gingerbread house together. It's a great test for future home renovation projects because you'll get a taste of the other person's design style. Do you really want to share a home with someone who thinks candy canes work as curtains?

CHRISTMAS

We shouldn't teach kids that being naughty or nice determines the gifts you receive in life. Be nice for the sake of being a decent human. Or, be a fucking dick because sometimes people deserve it. And, if you want cool presents, buy your own shit.

A lot of people joke about selling their soul to the Devil, but that's exactly what you're doing when you work for an employer who doesn't give a fuck about you. At least the Devil would throw some wild company parties; Sharon from HR would hate her job.

Spend too much time romanticizing other alternatives and you'll prevent yourself from finding purpose in your current reality. And, purpose is what fuels a strong mentality. Now, that purpose will be different for everyone, but what's really important is that you find one.

Sometimes, when you're
misunderstood, the best thing
you can do is become a missing
person. Not everyone deserves
an explanation, feel free to walk
away and keep on livin'.

Feeling offended is a fucking choice. The moment you let somebody else's words upset you, you've let somebody else defeat you. And, who the fuck wants to lose a battle to an opinion?

I appreciate people referring to themselves as a "snack." Because at least you know what to expect from them in terms of personality: a bag of chips. Somebody who's half empty and mostly just air.

Live the life that feels right — to you. What some people consider stability, you might consider monotony. What some people think is too kinky, you might think is necessary. And, when some people say, "This feels really risky," you'll say, "Damn, this really feels right."

NEW YEAR'S EVE

If somebody didn't choose you this
year, let them completely fucking lose
you next year. Once somebody has
made up their mind, have the self-
respect to stop wasting your own time.

ABOUT THE AUTHOR

Writer. Creator. Instigator. Not your dad.

@SGRSTK

Made in the USA
Las Vegas, NV
07 November 2023

80406772R00203